am and Kim were riding along the roa(

They saw Dan's mum. She was looking

1

"Have you seen Dan?" she said. "He's late for tea. He isn't in th
house and he isn't in the garden. He's *never* late for tea!"

Kim and Sam shook their heads.

"No, we haven't seen him anywhere," said Sam, "but we'll go and look for him."

They rode off to look for Dan.

They rode past Kev.

"Have you seen Dan?" said Sam. "He's late for tea. He isn't in the house and he isn't in the garden."

Kev shook his head.

"No," he said, "I haven't seen him anywhere. See if he's up on the hill. He's always playing up there."

Sam and Kim rode up to the hill but they couldn't see Dan anywhere.

"I hope he's OK," said Kim.

Then Info-rider's screen began to flash.

Sound coming from the hut!" flashed the screen. "Sound coming
·om the hut!"

 can't hear a sound, can you?" said Kim.

No, I can't hear a sound," said Sam. "Let's go and look."

They rode over to the hut.

"Sh!" said Kim. "What's that?"

Someone was calling for help.

"It's Dan!" said Sam.

"I *know* it's me!" said Dan. "Get me out of here! The door's stuck!"

am and Kim pulled and pulled at the door, but it wouldn't open.
They tugged and tugged at the door, but it still wouldn't open.
It won't open at all," said Sam. "It's stuck fast."

"Try to open the window, Dan," said Kim.
"I've tried and tried to open the window," said Dan. "But it won't open. It's stuck fast, too."

It's no good," said Sam. "The door won't open. The window won't open. What shall we do?"

Just then Info-rider's screen began to flash.

"Get the chain," the screen said. "Get the chain."

"Where will I find a chain?" said Sam.
The screen flashed again.
"Look at the back of the hut," it said. "Look at
the back of the hut."
"Go and see if you can find a chain, Sam," said Kim.

Sam went to the back of the hut. He found a chain by some old boxes.

"I've found one, Kim," he said. "I've found one!"

The screen flashed again.

"Put one end of the chain over the seat," it said.

Sam put one end of the chain over the seat.

The screen flashed again.
'Put the other end of the chain over the door handle," it said.
Kim put the other end of the chain over the door handle.

"I still don't see how this is going to work," said Kim.
"It will work," said Sam. "Info-rider can do anything. Just wait and see."

The screen flashed again.

"Tell Dan to keep away from the door," it said.

"Keep away from the door, Dan," said Sam.

"OK," said Dan.

Sam got on Info-rider. The screen flashed.

"Power on. Power on," it said. "Stand by. Stand by."

"Wow," said Sam, "this is going to be good."

"Ride fast, Sam," flashed the screen. "*Ride fast!*"
Sam rode as fast as he could.
The door did not move.

"The door isn't moving!" said Kim.
"Power boost needed. Power boost needed," said the screen.
"What's a power boost?" said Sam.

he screen flashed red. It had a big orange dot on it.
Press the orange dot for power boost," flashed the screen.
am pressed the orange dot.

The bike began to shake.

"Ride fast, Sam," flashed the screen. "Ride fast!"

Sam rode faster and faster. The door began to move.

The door's moving!" said Kim. "Keep going, Sam! Keep going!" The door moaned and groaned. It creaked and squeaked. Then, with a loud crack, it shot open!

Sam braked hard. He braked so hard that he left deep, deep marks on the ground. Kim ran to the hut to get Dan. "Just in time!" said Dan. "I have to go home for my tea!"